Peggy Louise Parrish
Parma, Idaho 83660
All writing and artwork on cover and in the interior
By Peggy Louise Parrish

ISBN-13:978-1543197112
Printed in The United States of America

The Quaint Letter Q

Coloring Book

By Peggy Louise Parrish

C. 2017

Dear Coloring Artists,

Welcome to a unique coloring experience with over 20 Q Letter designs. These pages are filled with interesting Q Letters just waiting to be colored by you. The colors you choose and the art medium you choose will give each letter your artistic touch. Quality colored pencils are the preferred medium of choice. However, ink gel pens, watercolor pencils, markers, or paint can be used successfully if you place a piece of scrap paper under your work.

Perhaps your first or last name begins with the letter Q. If so you will really enjoy some new Q designs. Just for fun settle in somewhere to relax with your colors and these pages. You may make a few "in house" copies of the pages you want to color different ways. If you want to print up a few copies of your color work for yourself or a gift you may. Remember to keep the artist initials on the bottom and not to sell anything from this book. May you use this book to excite yourself with all the letter possibilities yet to be designed and colored.

If you find this book rewarding the other 25 letters of the alphabet have their own books in this series.

Color till your heart's content.

Welcome to the Quaint Letter Q!

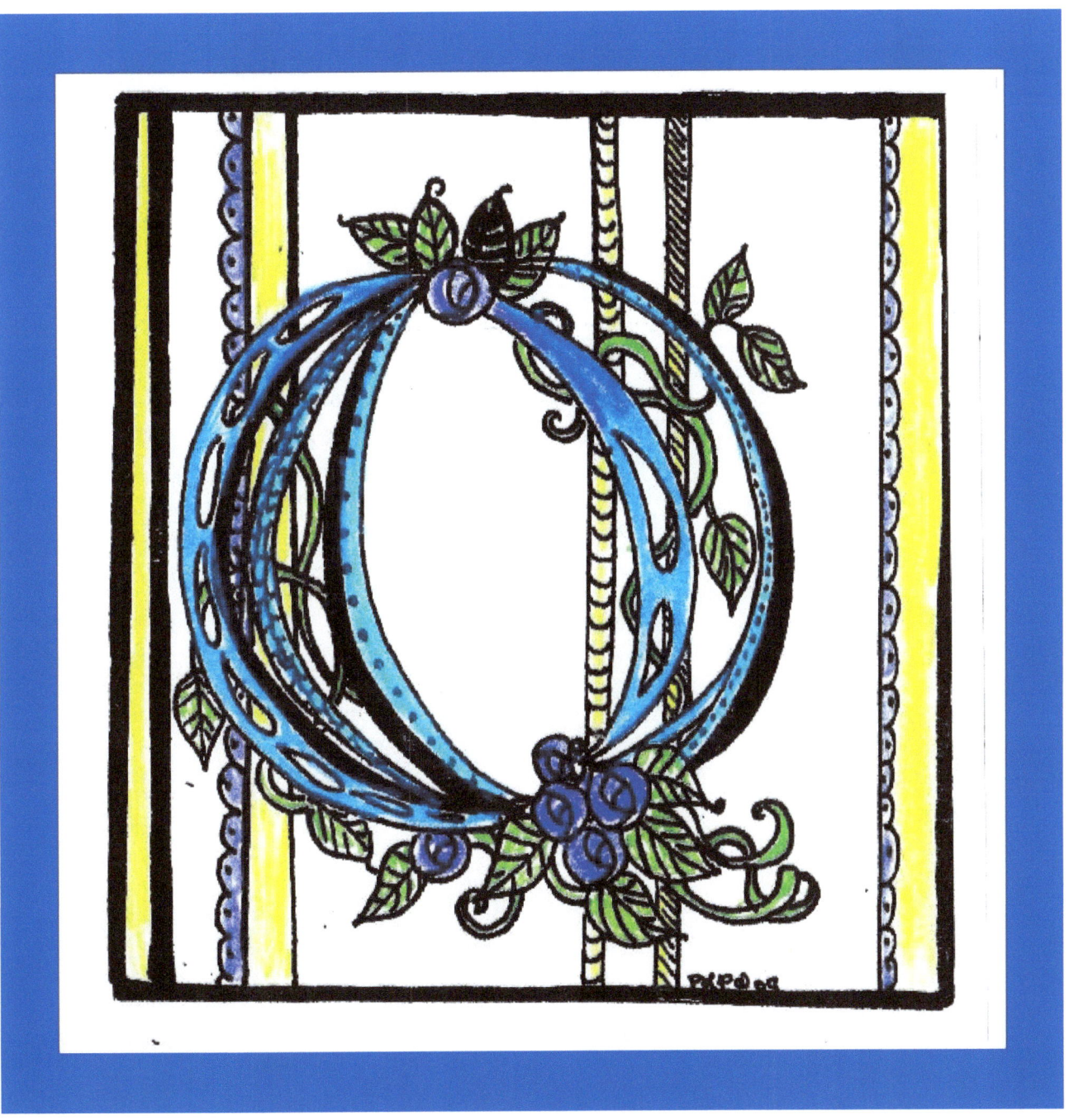

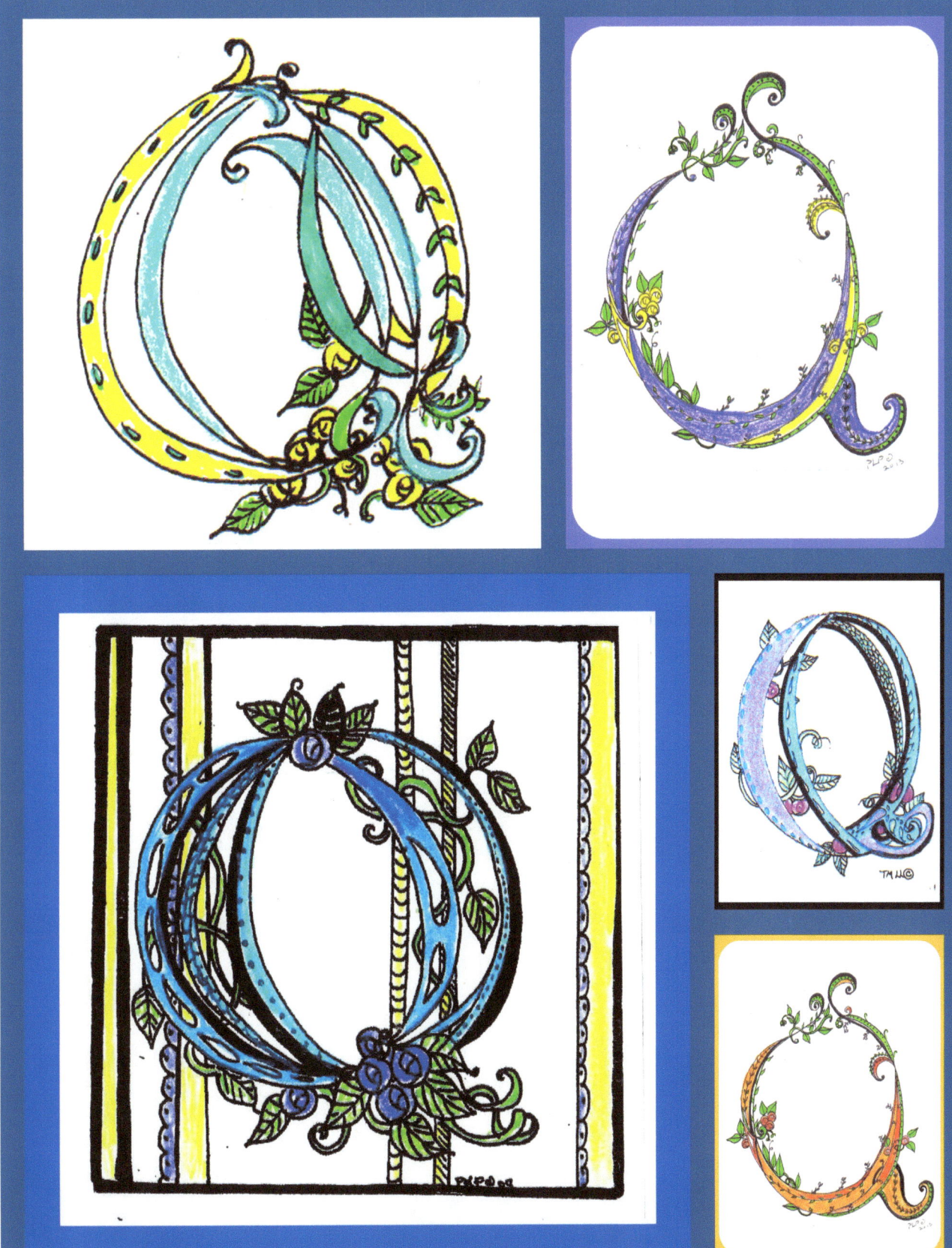

The
Quaint
Q

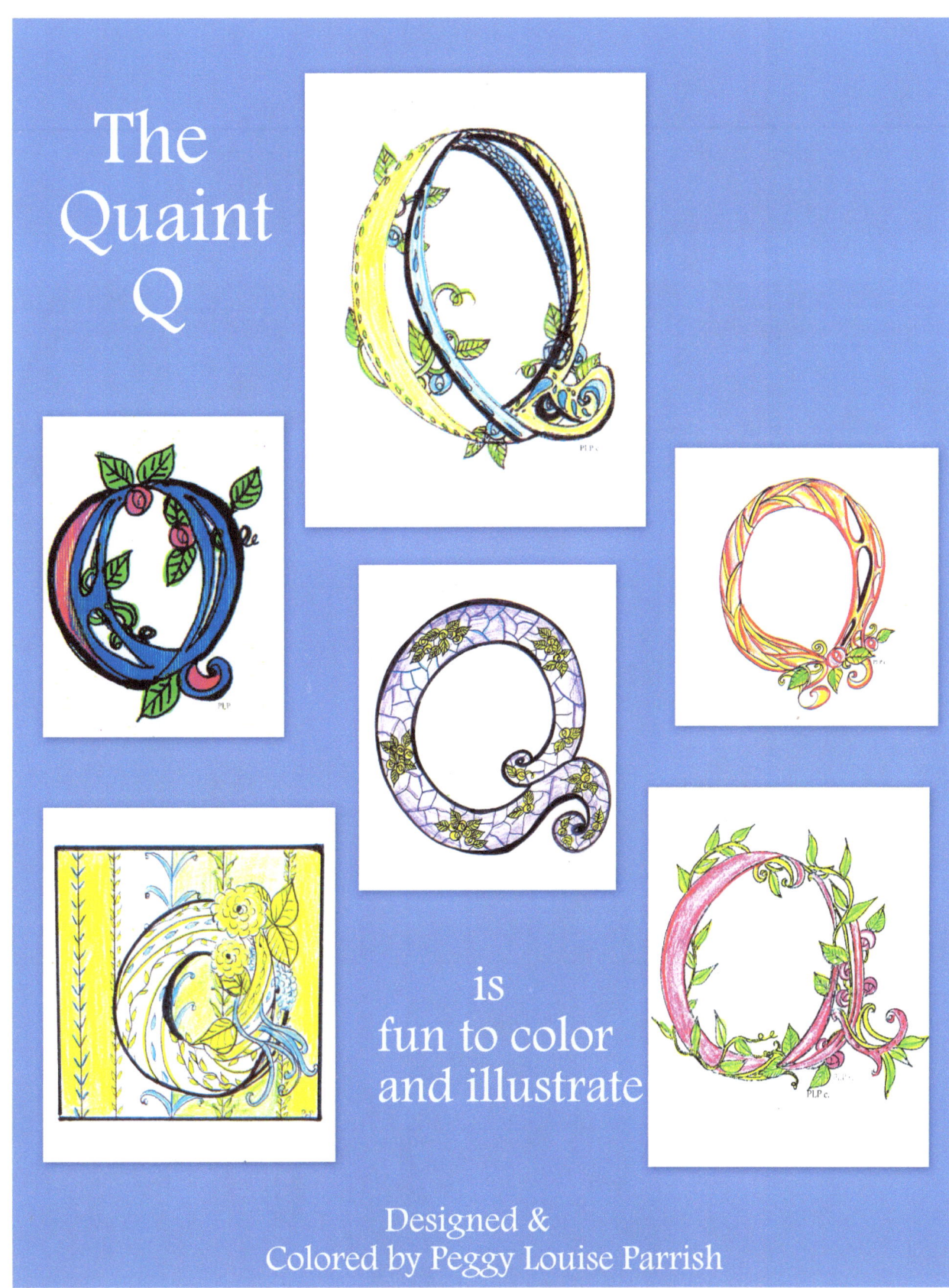

is
fun to color
and illustrate

Designed &
Colored by Peggy Louise Parrish

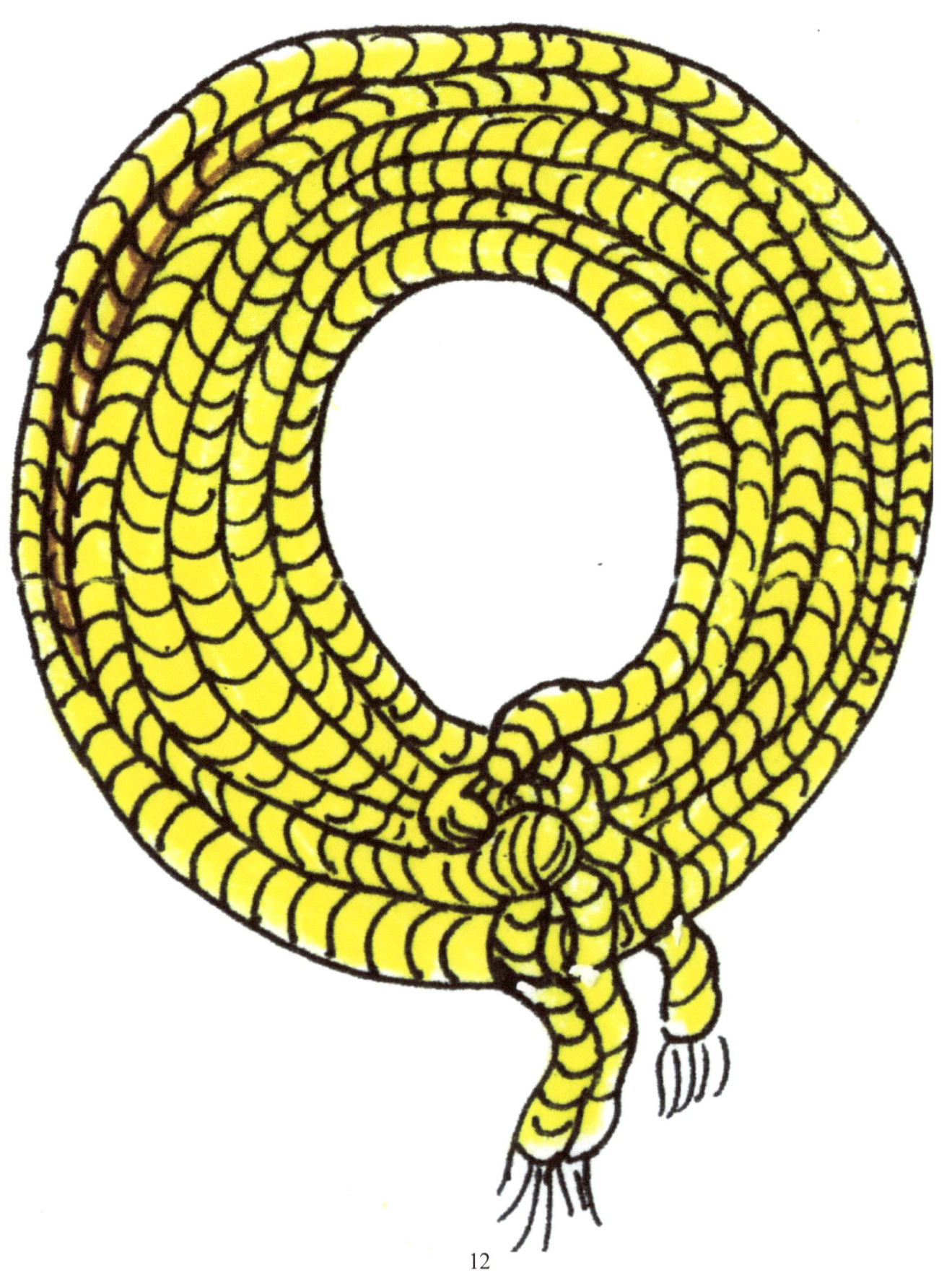

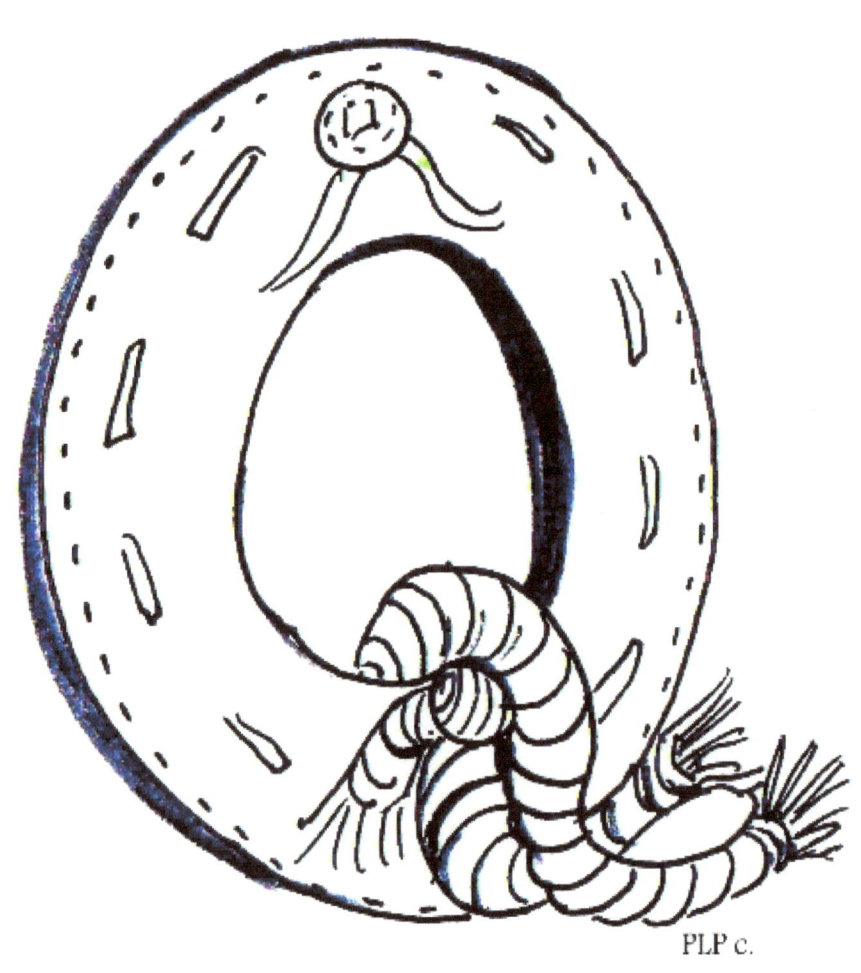

PLP c.

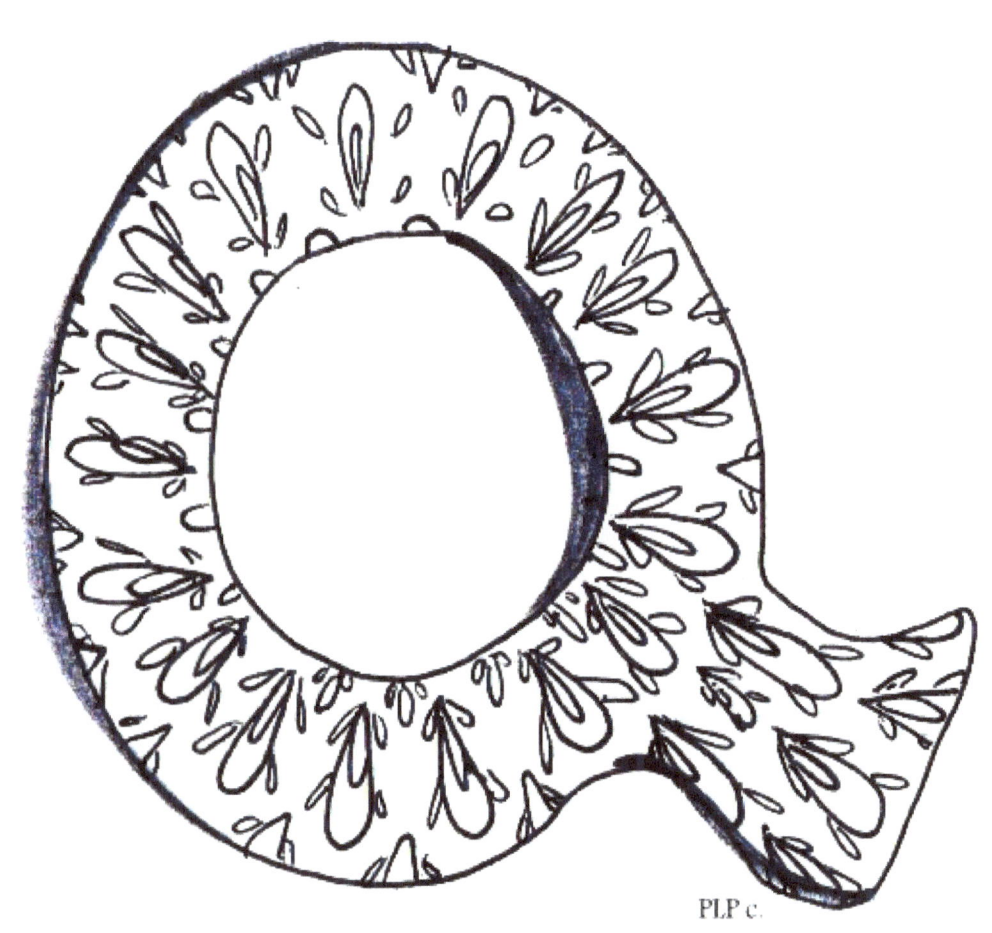

PLP c.

15

What color do you want this cowboy rope Q to be?

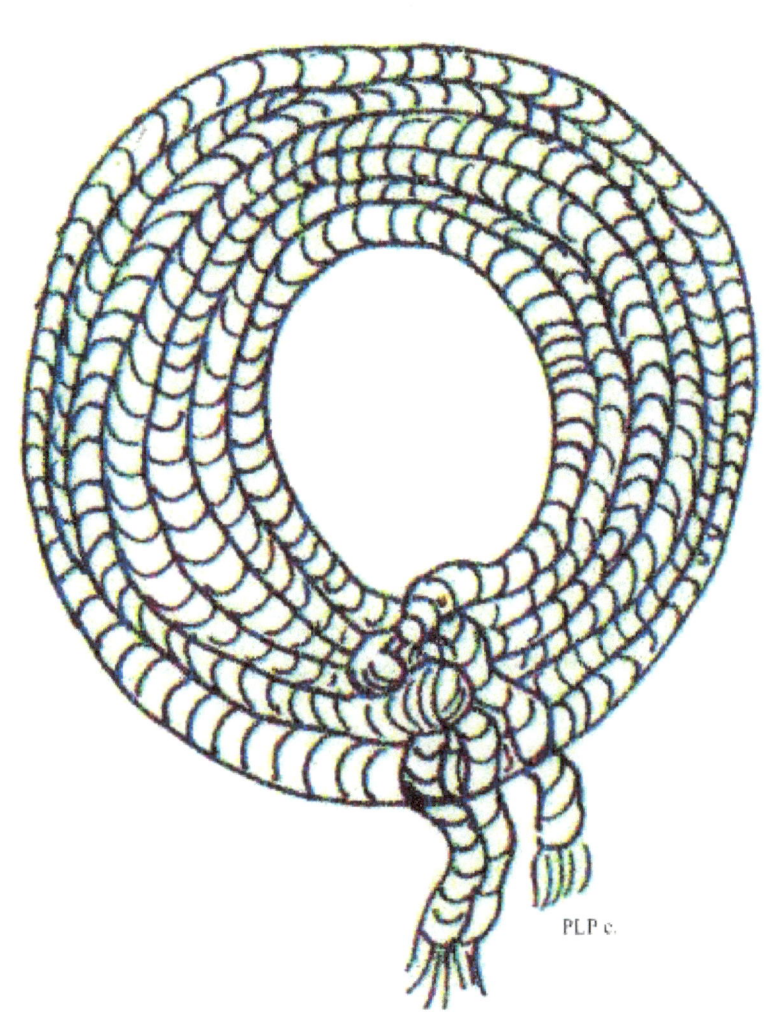

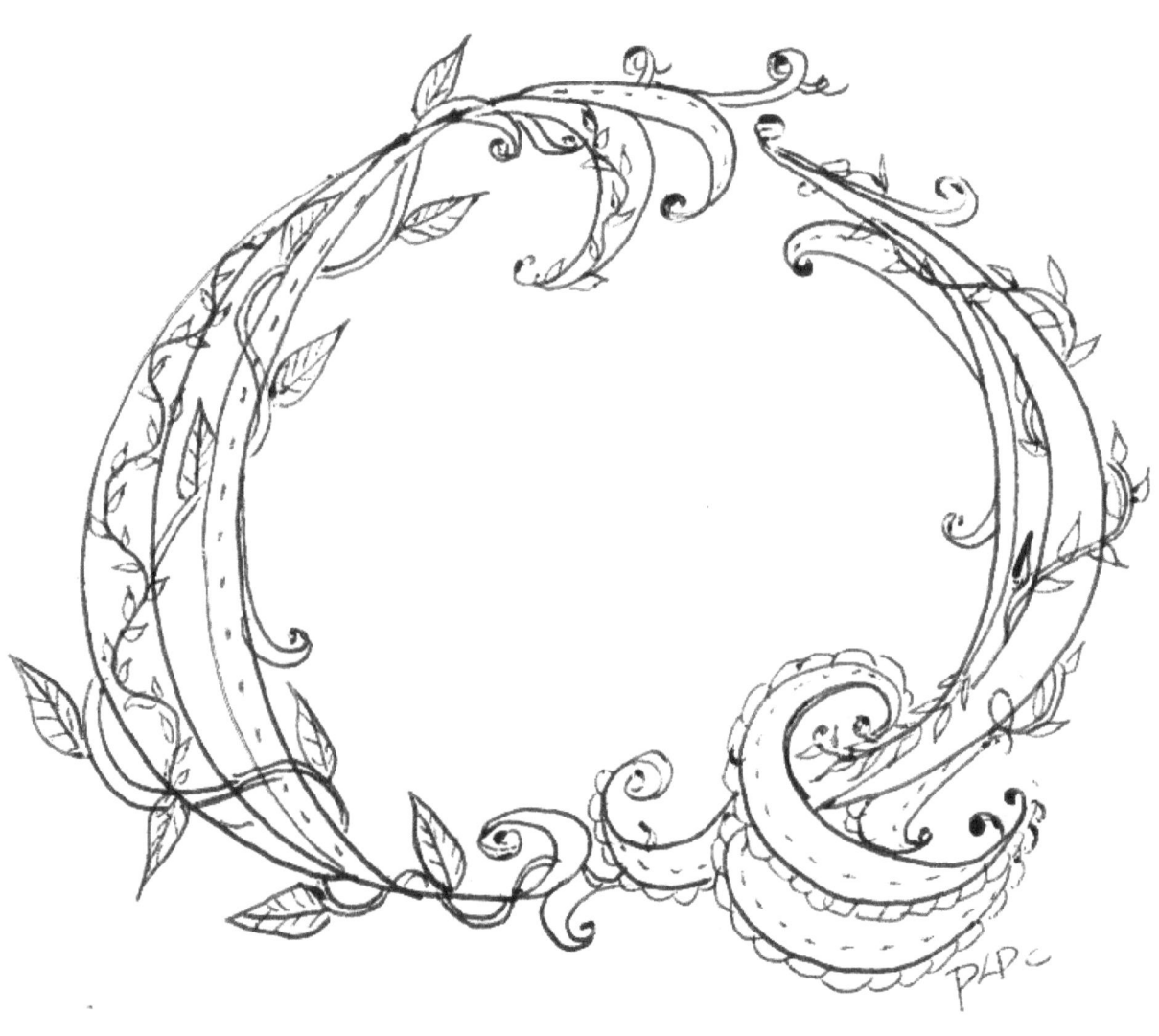

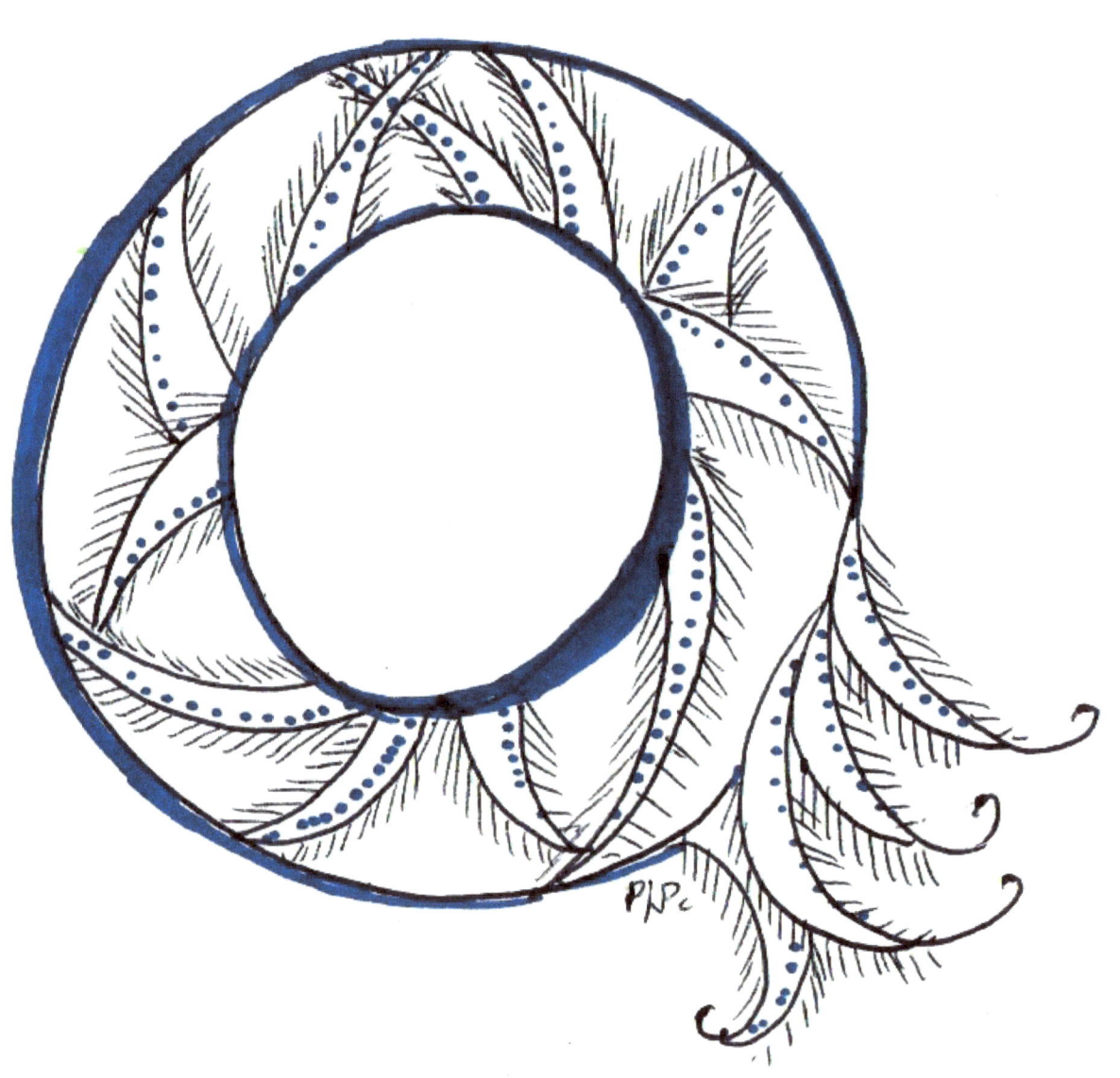

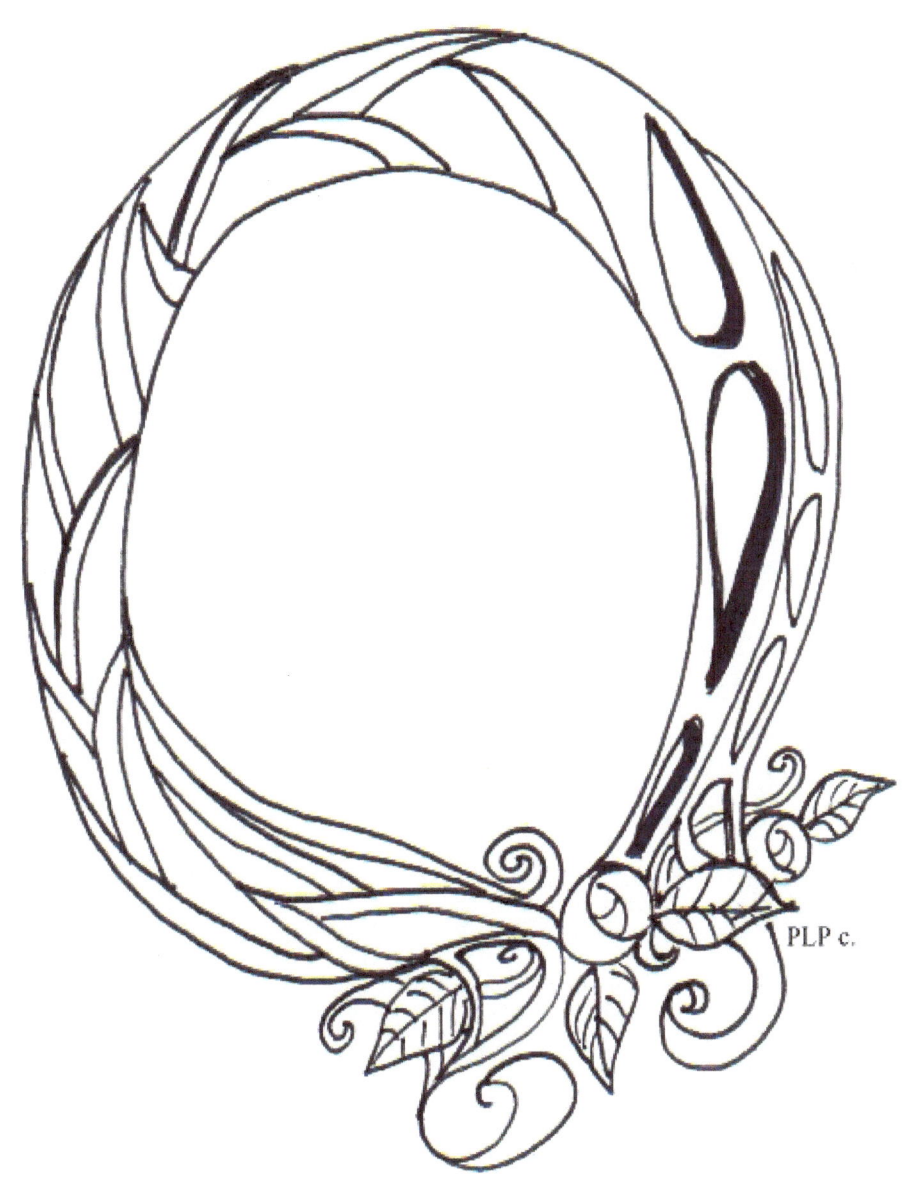

PLP c.

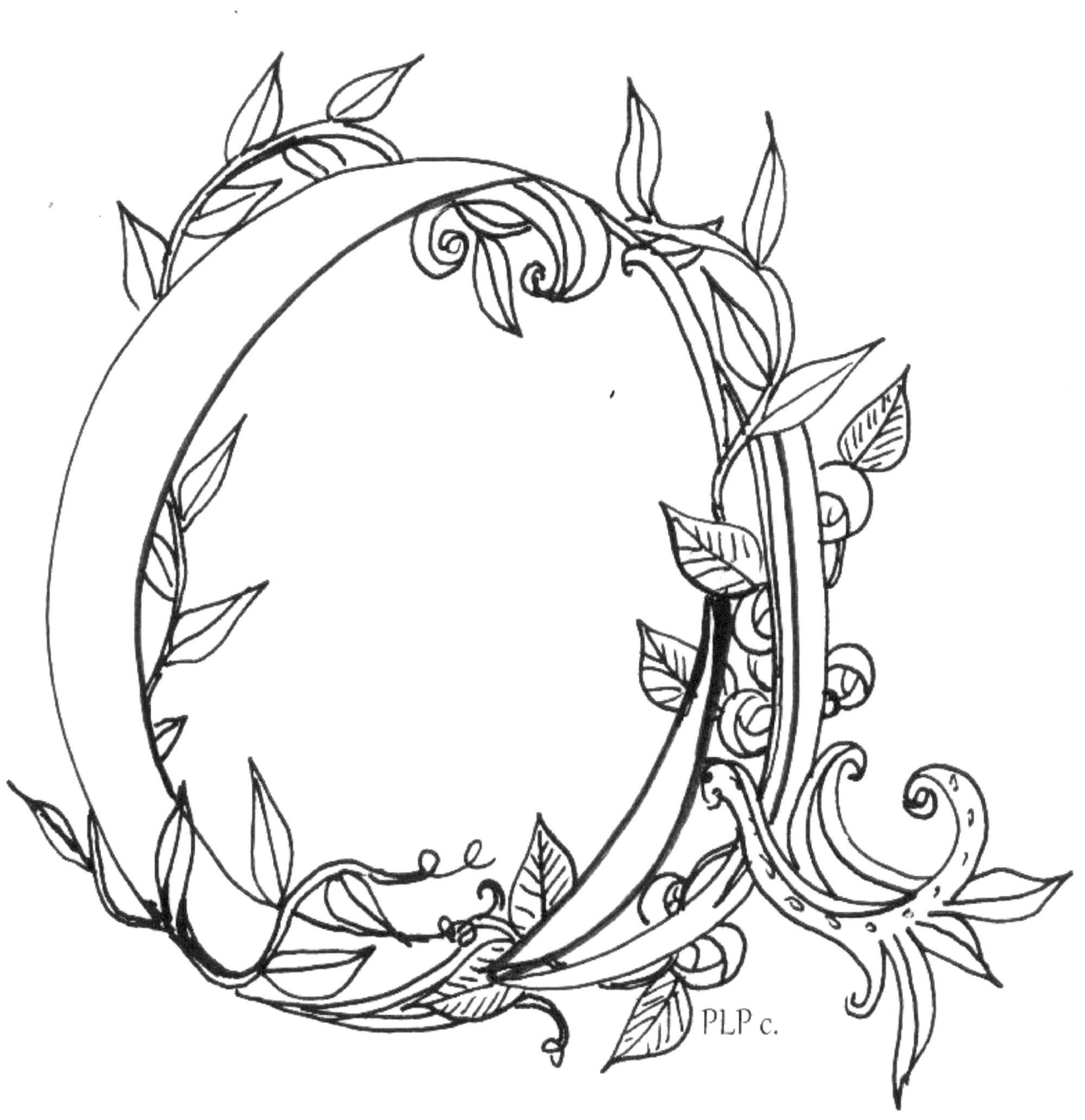

PLP c.

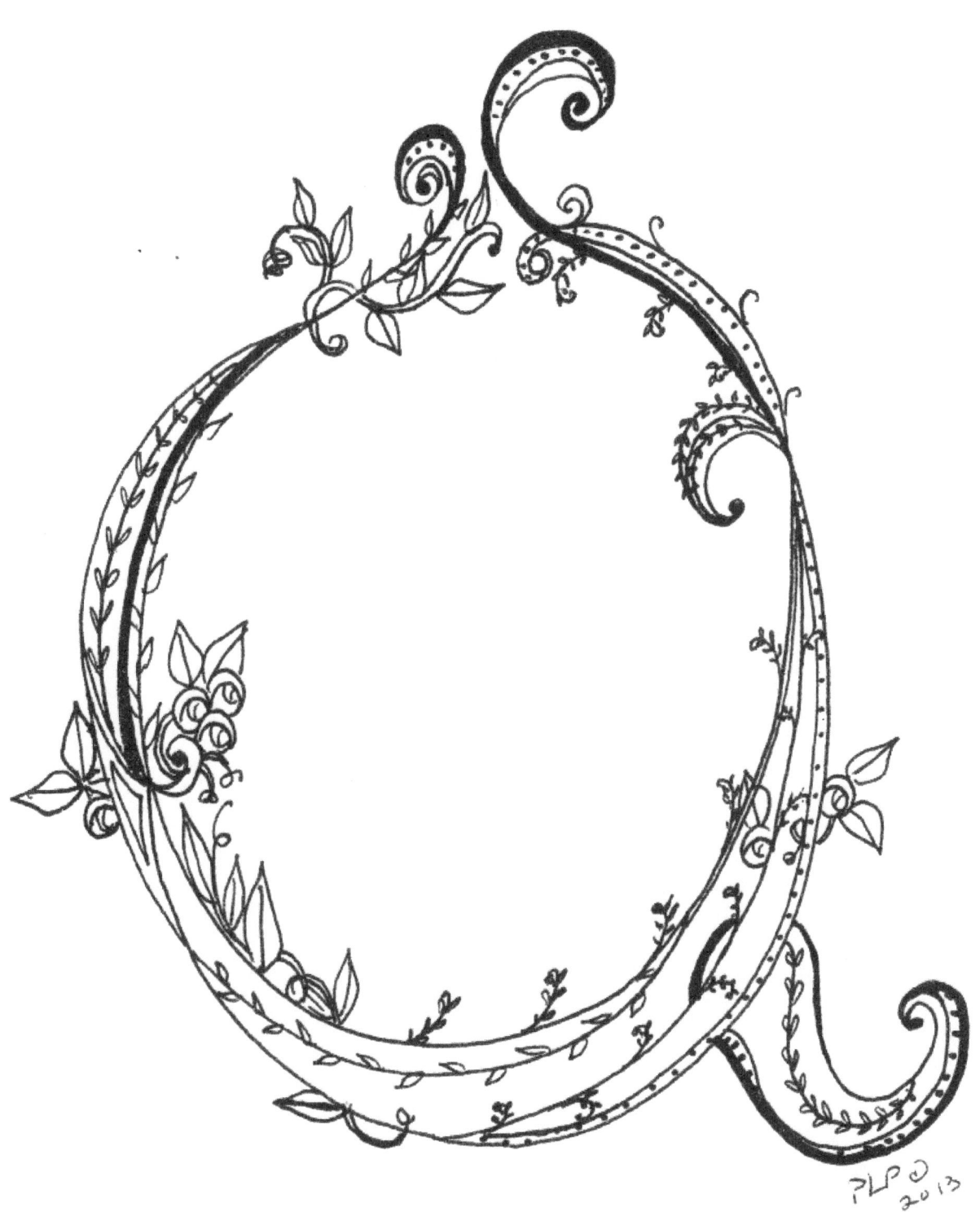

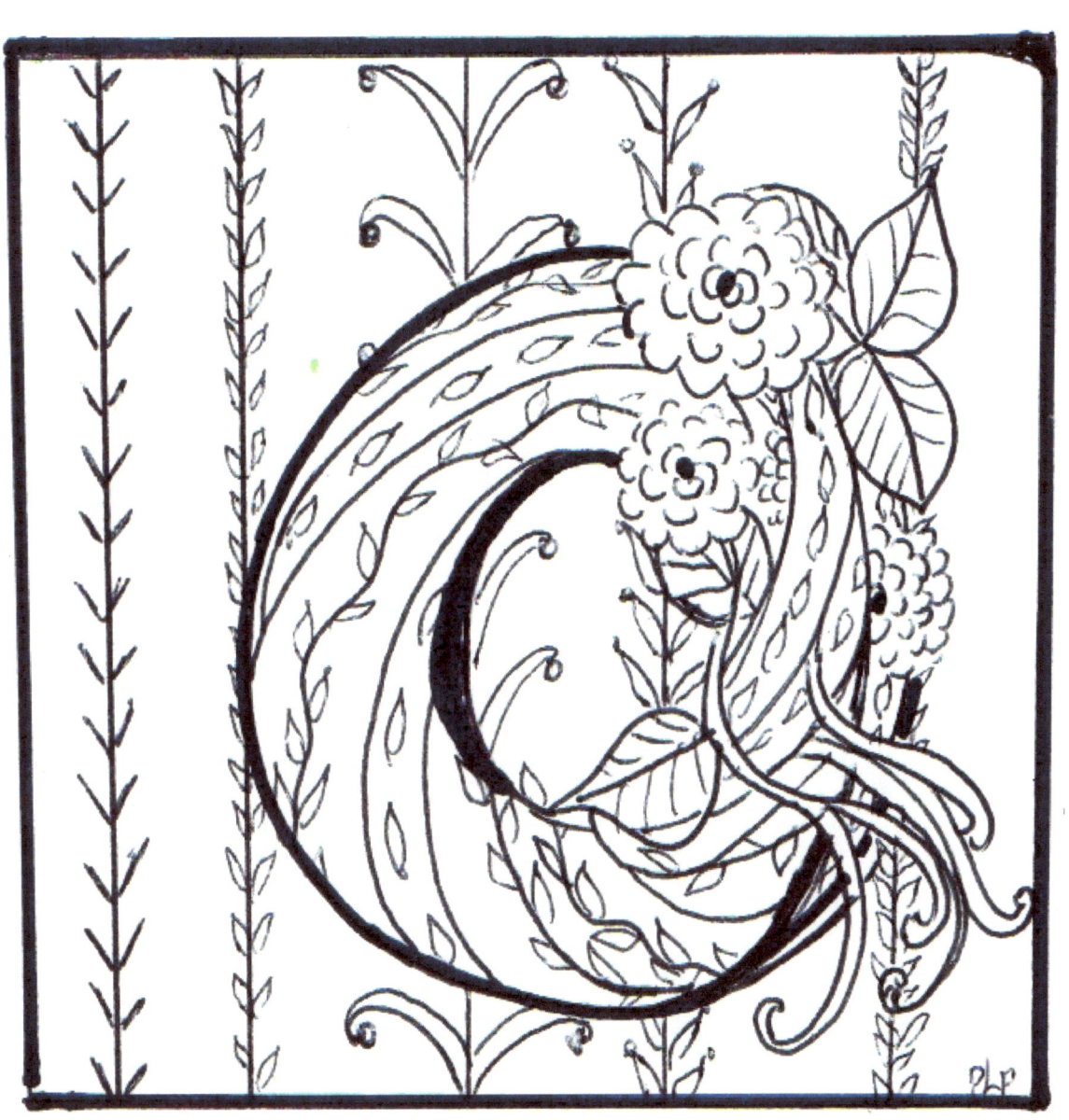

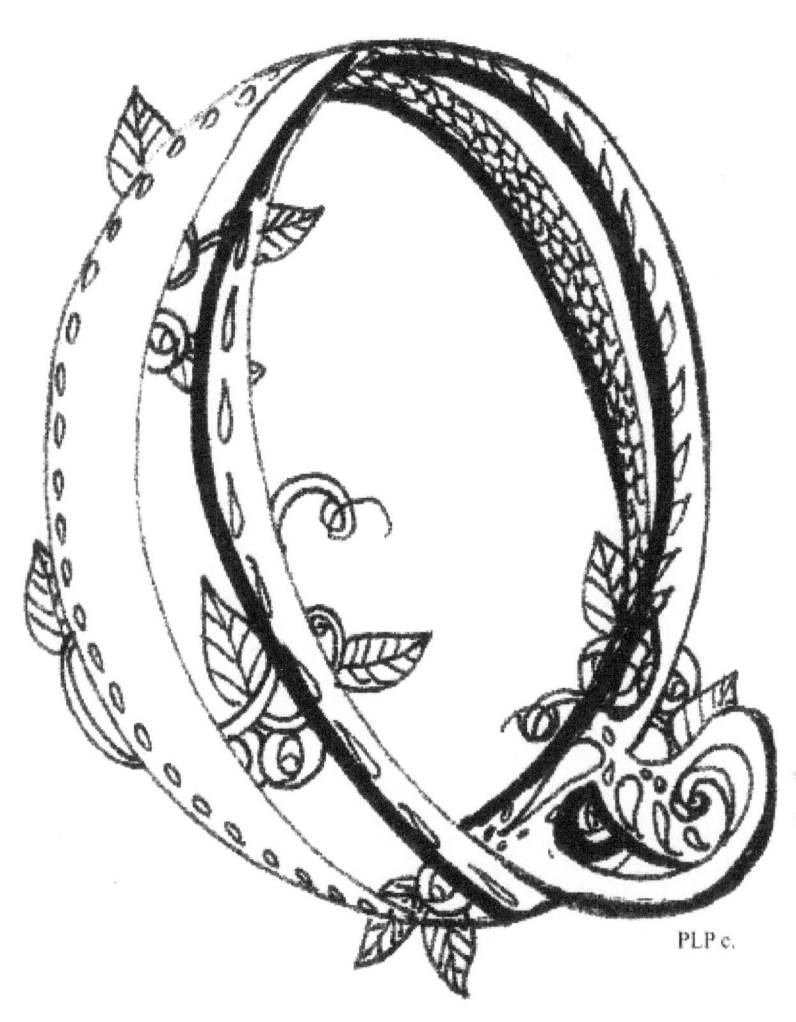

PLP c.

31

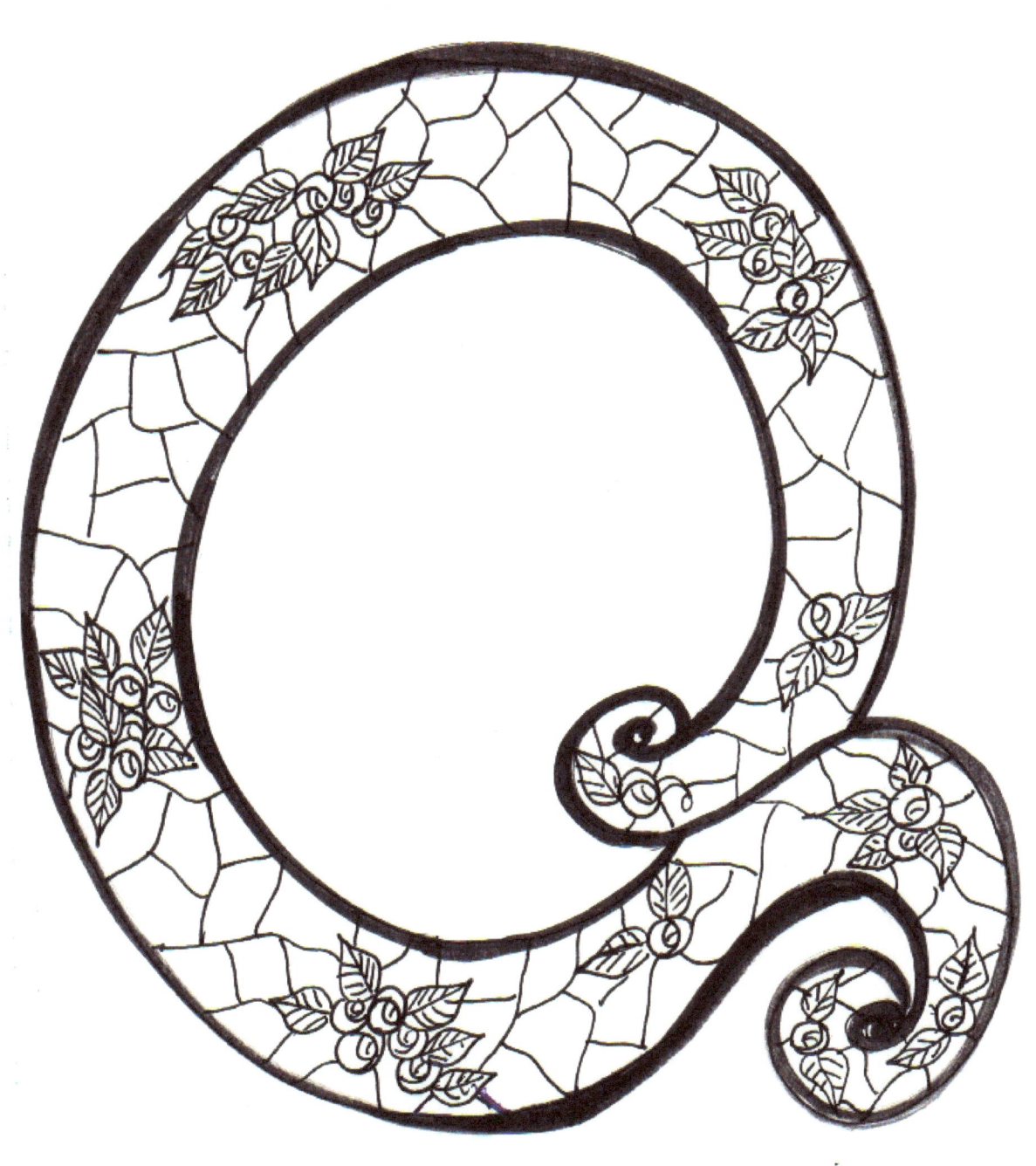

PLP C. 2013

33

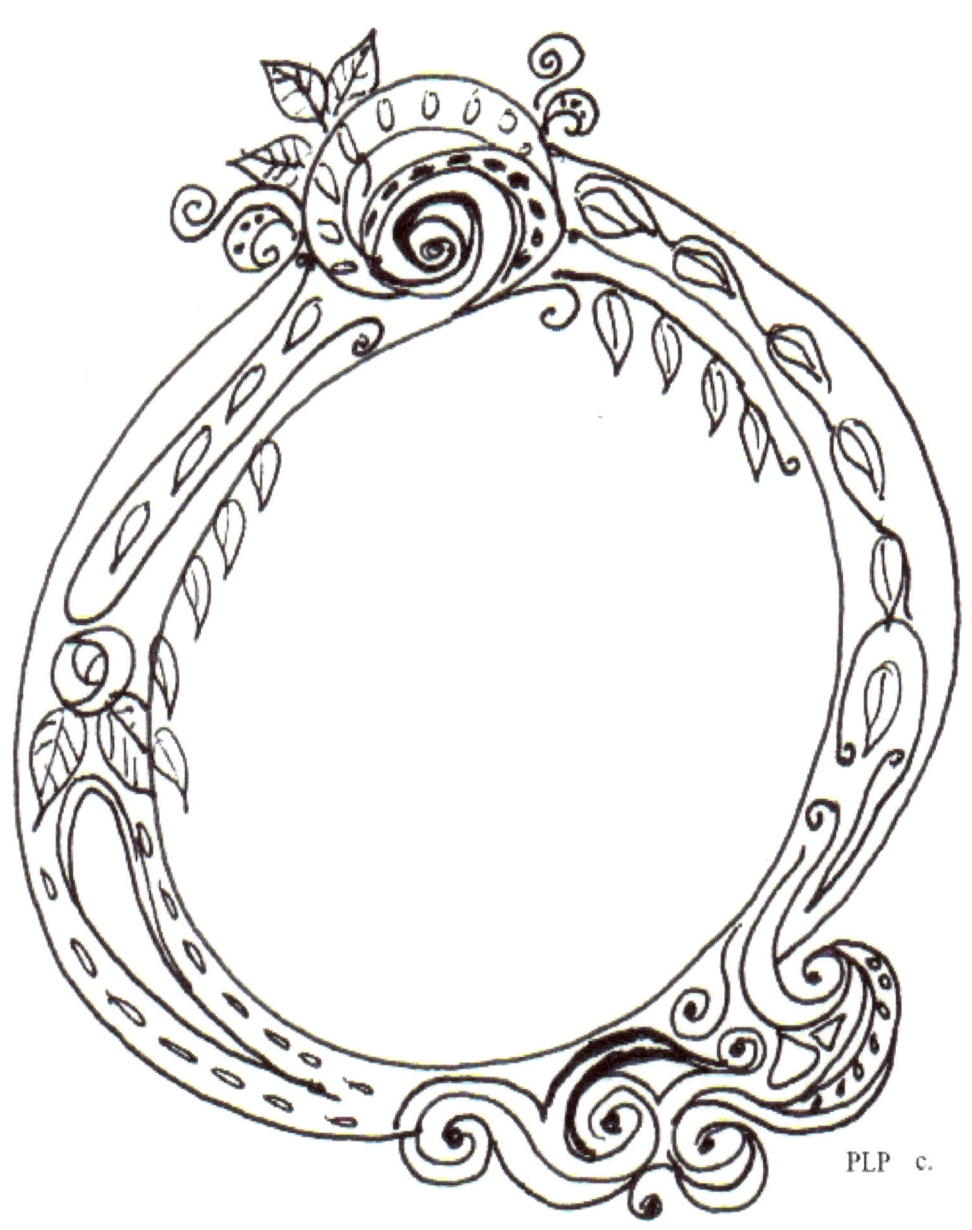

PLP c.

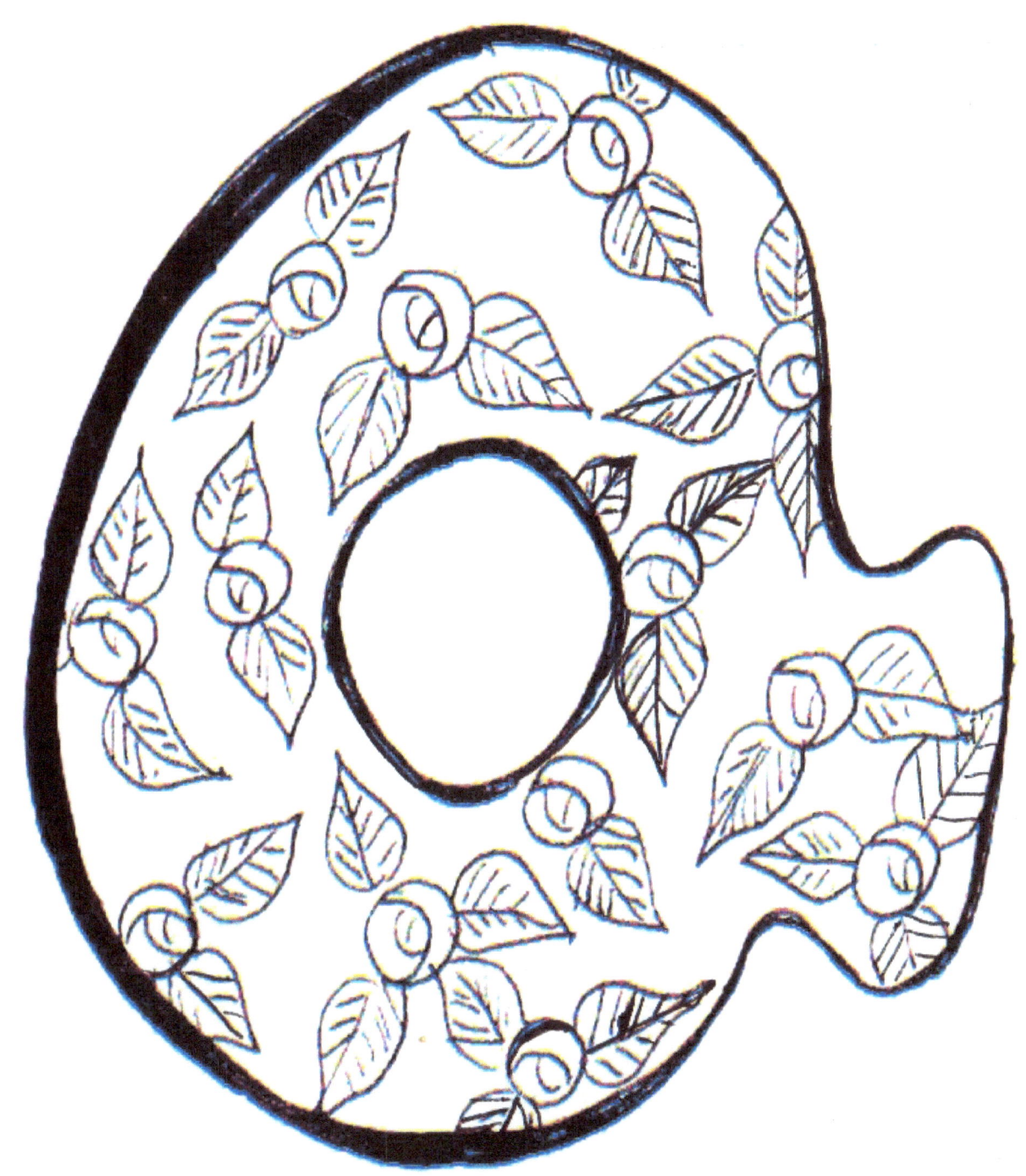

PLP c.

PLP c.

PLP c.

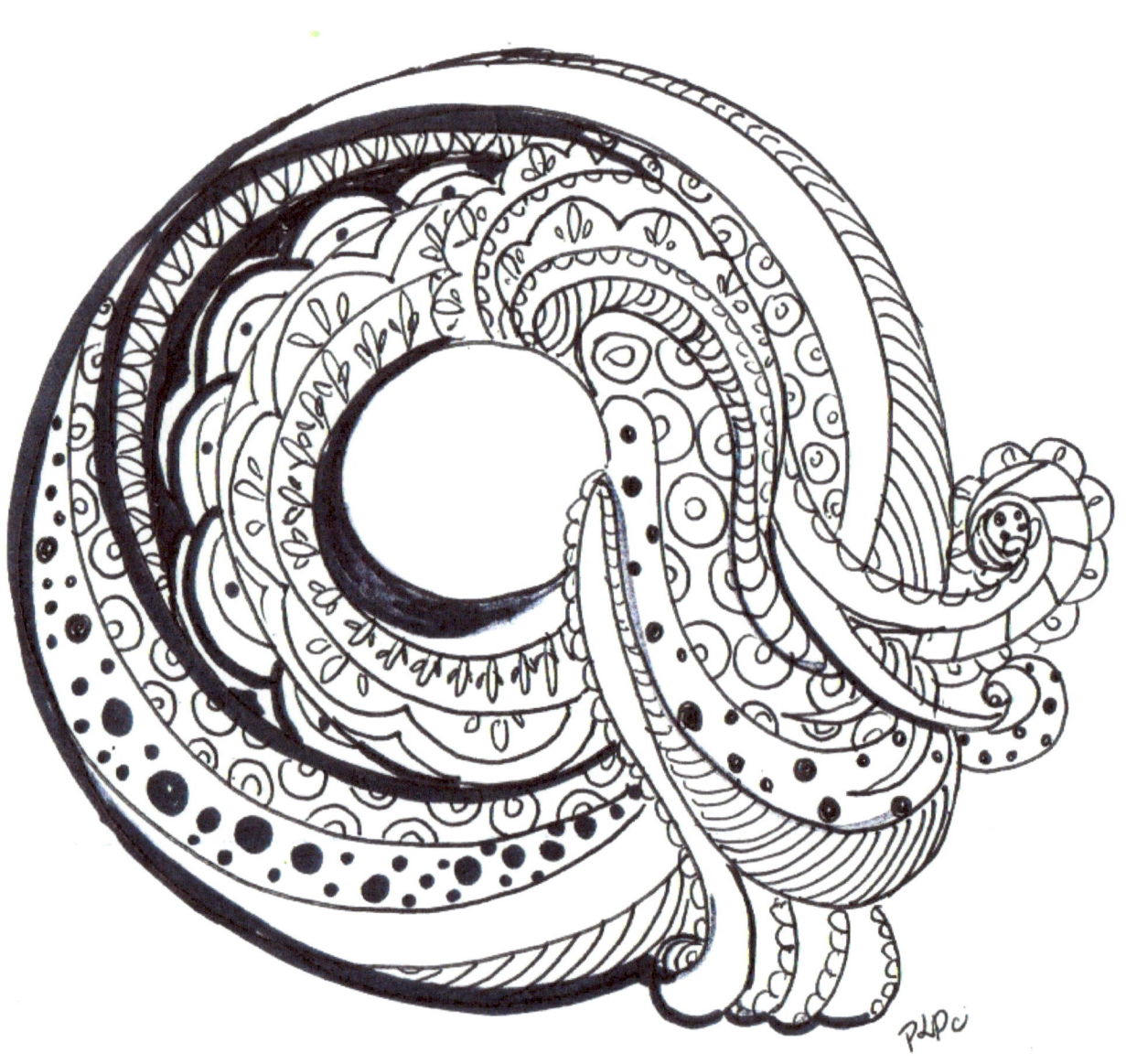

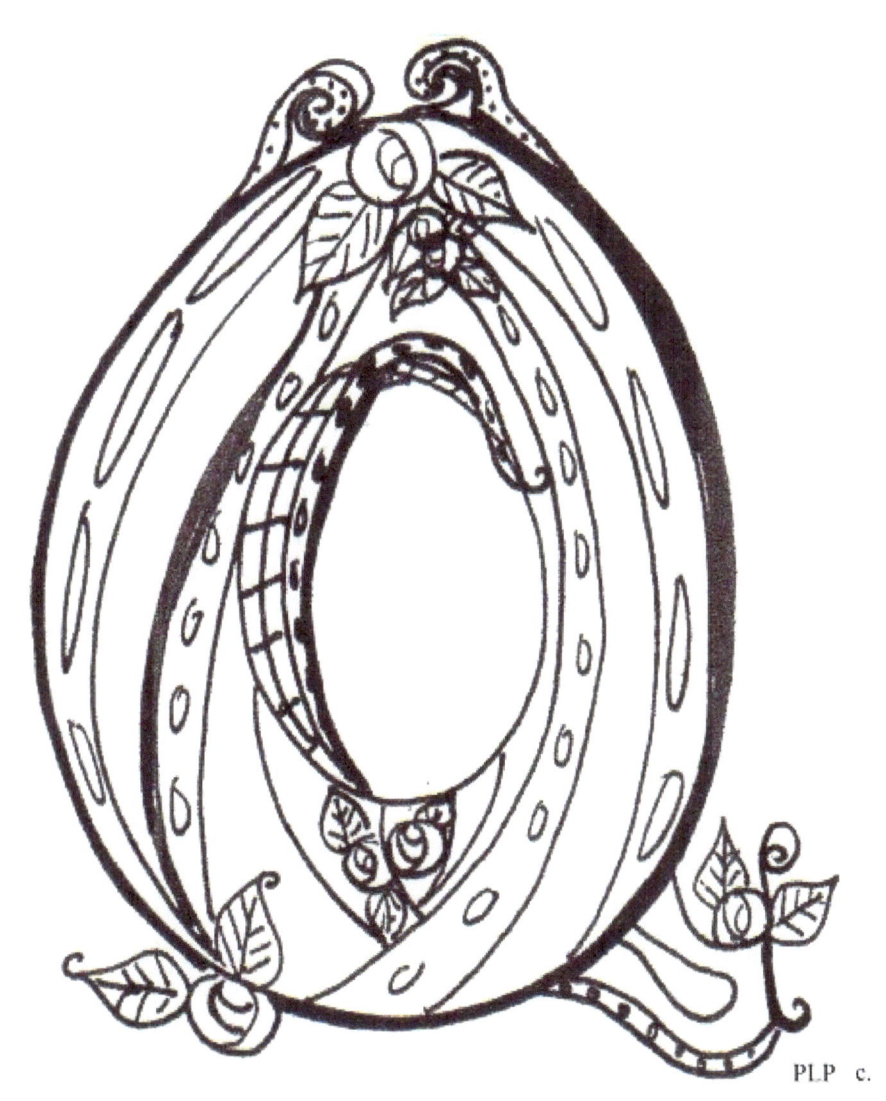

PLP c.

47

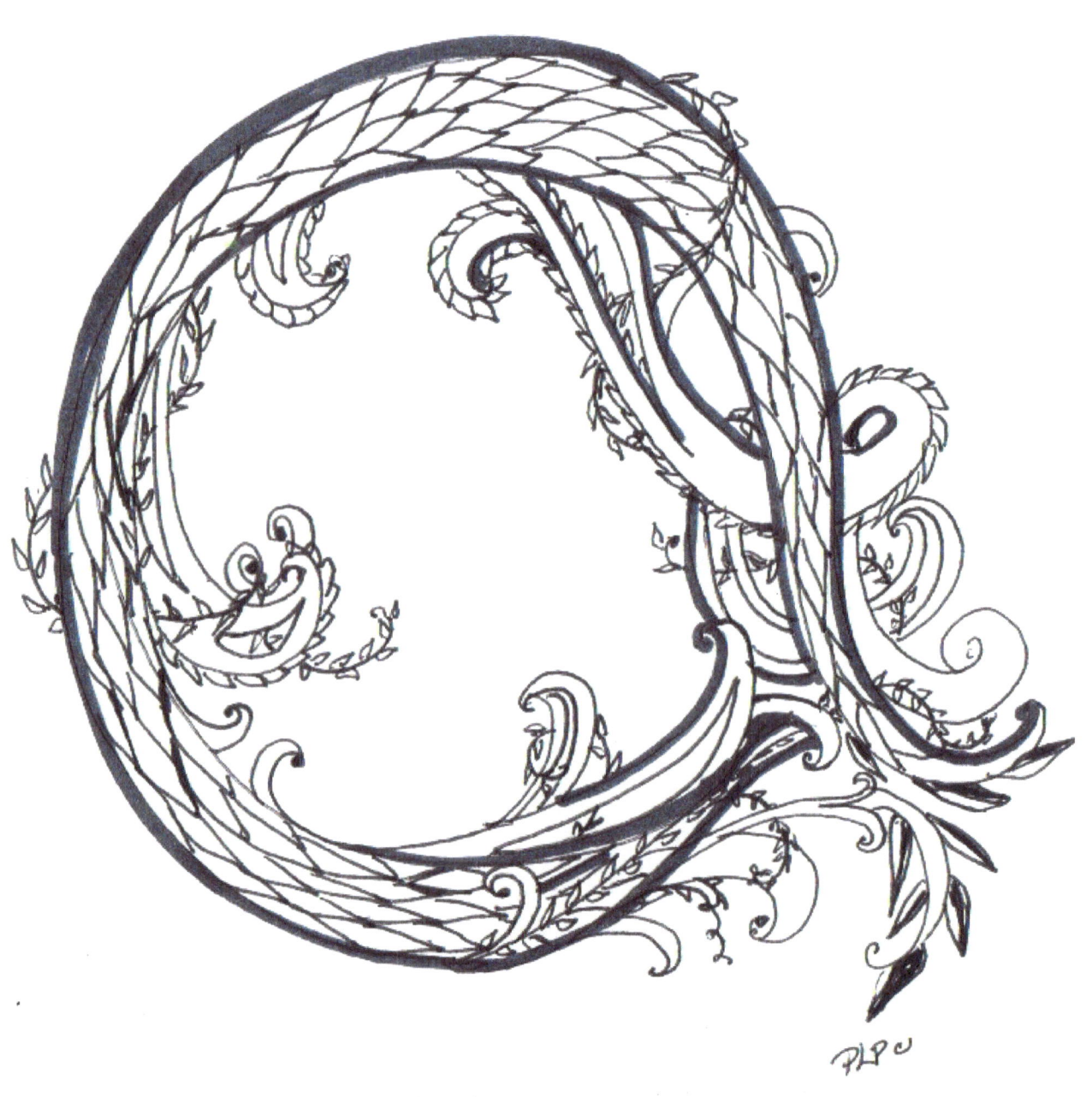

Letter Q can be made of ribbons and growing plants.

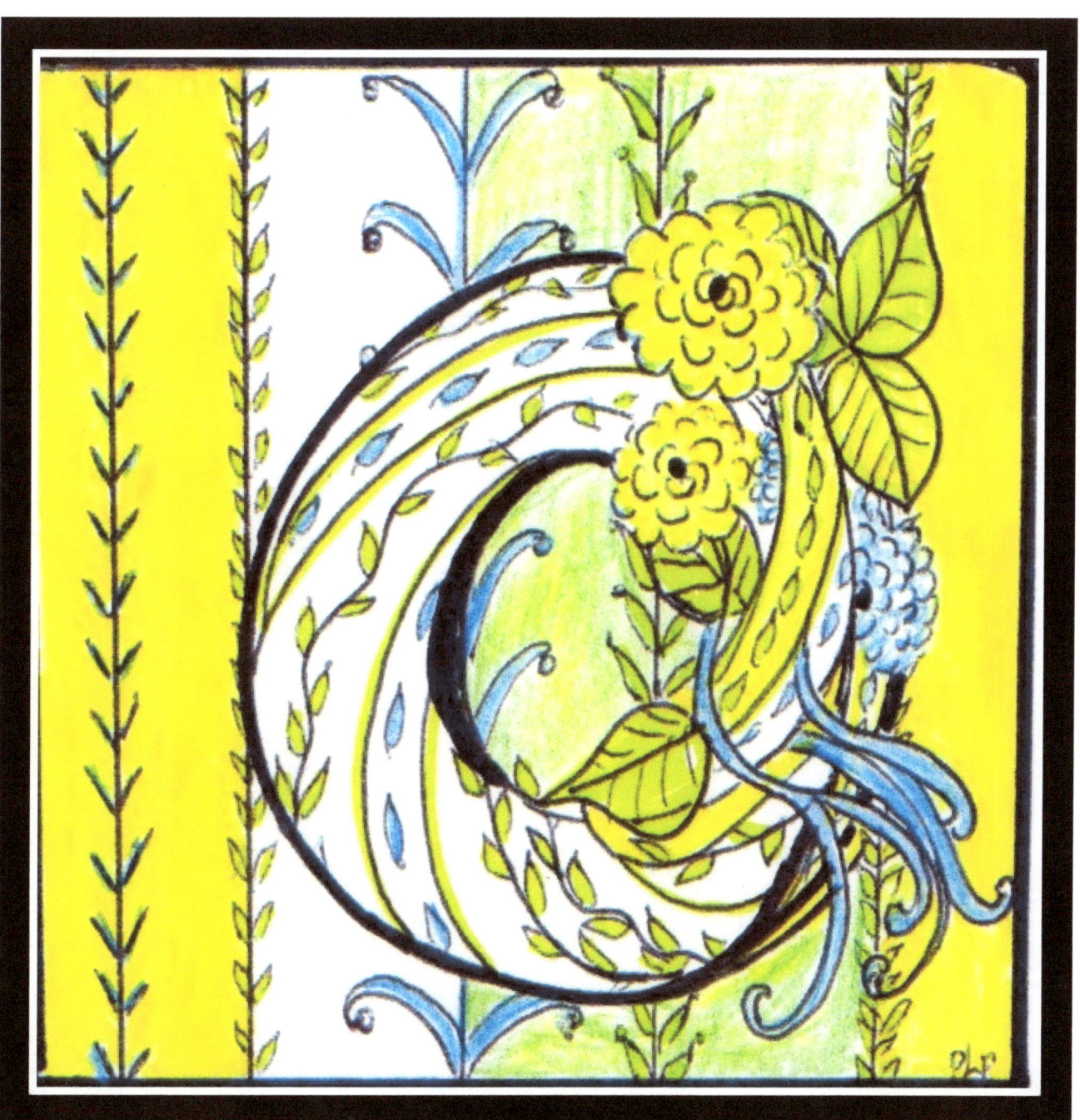

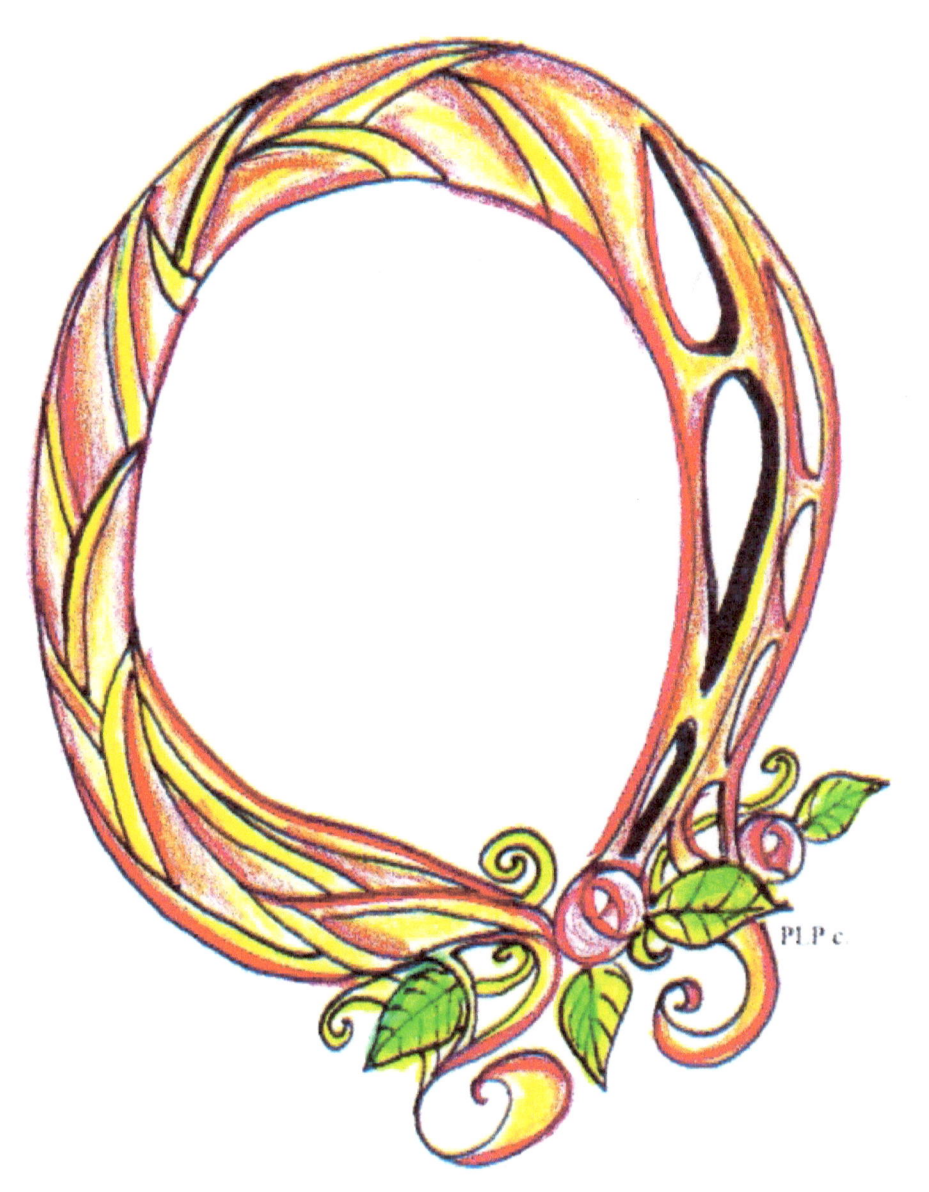

Q can be so cute!

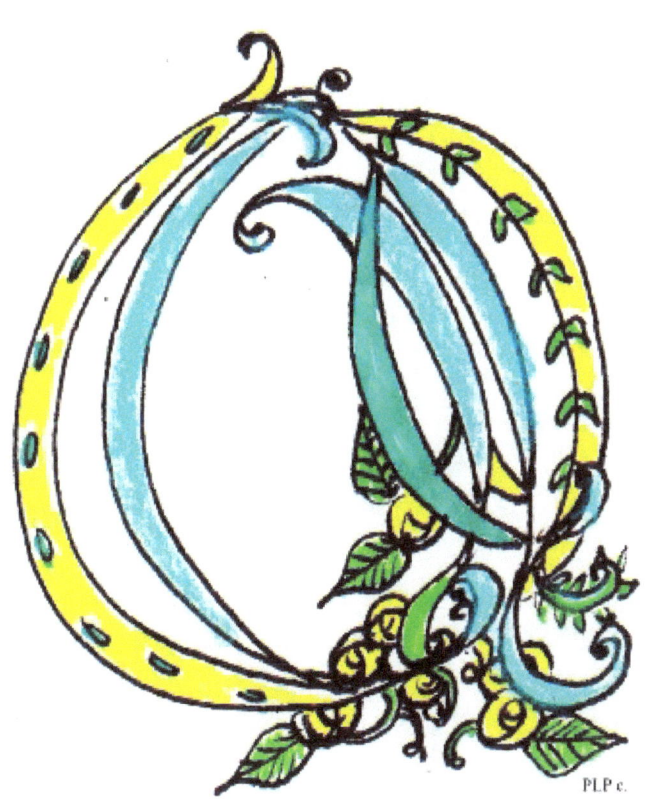

This Q shows possible sewing designs. Can you try to make one of your own?

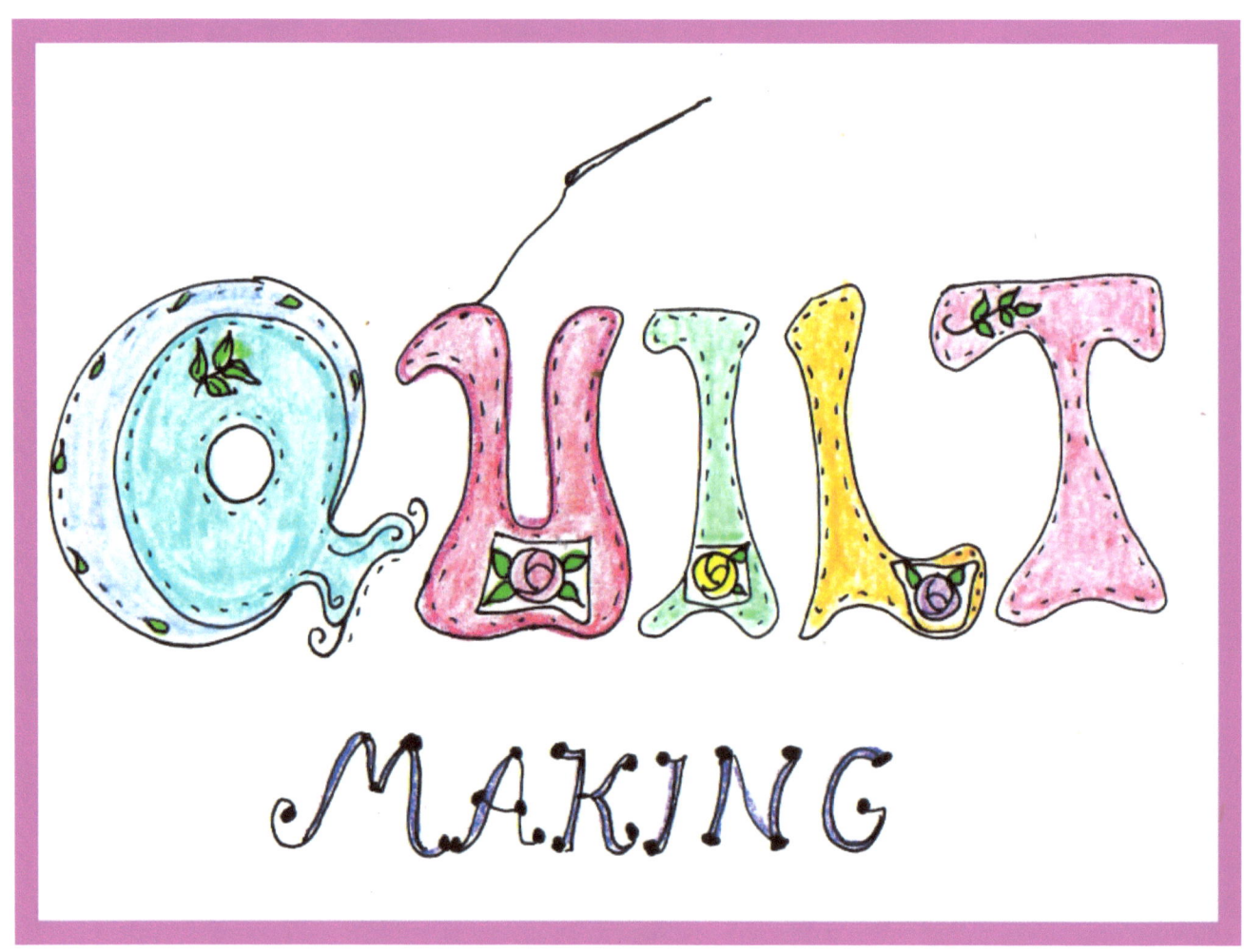

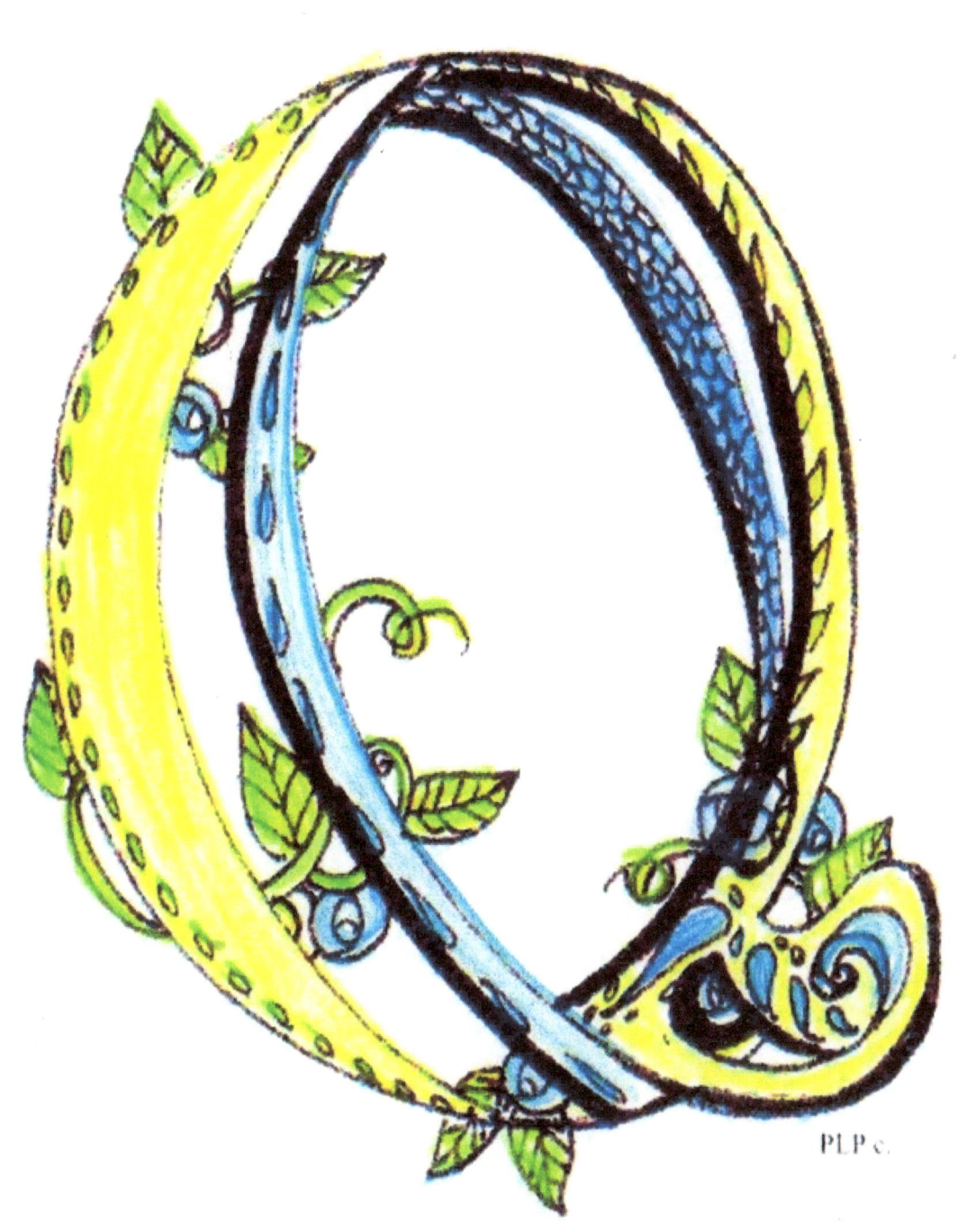

PLP c.

Hopefully you have had a wonderful Q adventure in this book. Try the other Wonder Letter Coloring Books by artist Peggy Louise Parrish. Just think how fun the other letters can be to color as well.

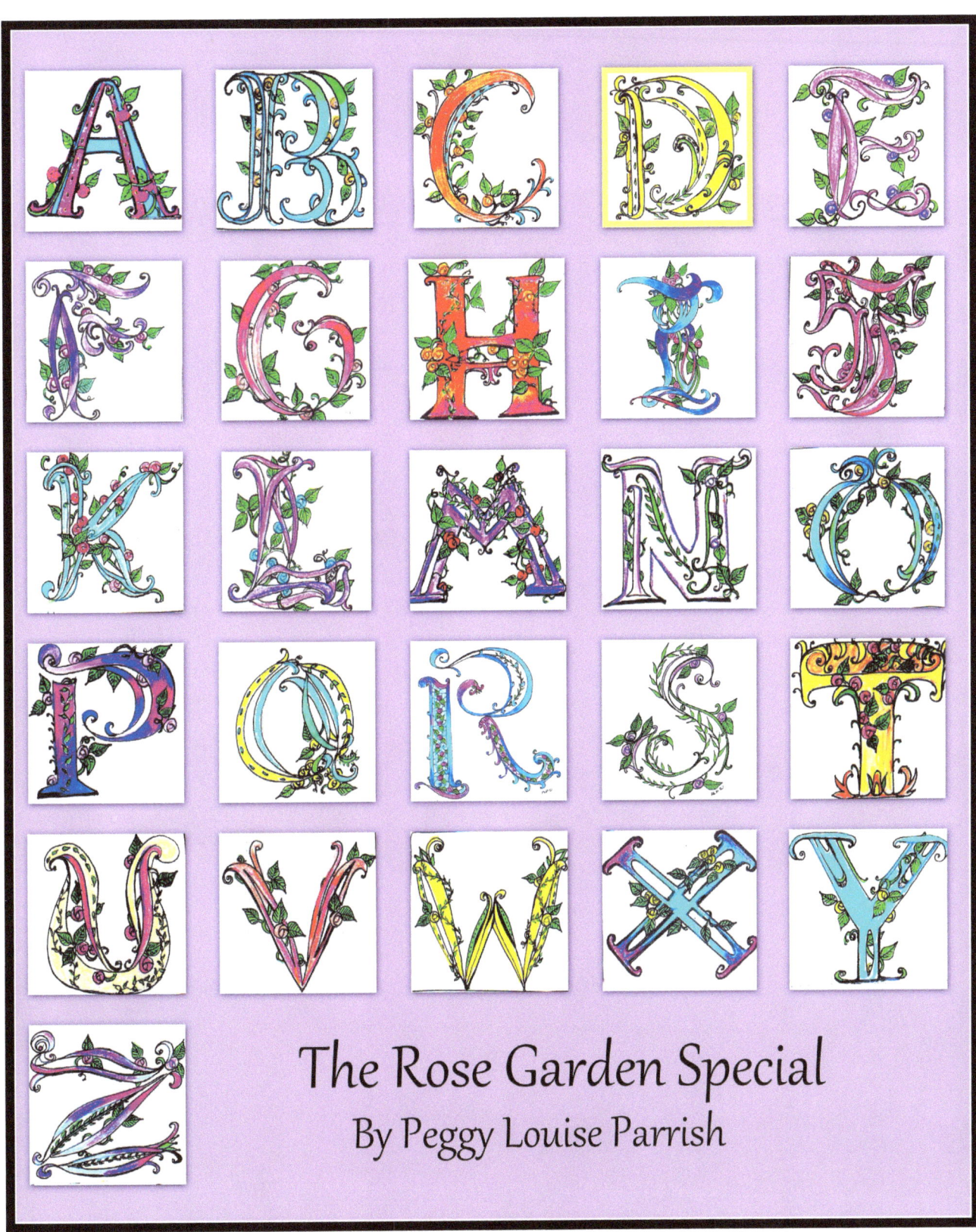

The Rose Garden Special
By Peggy Louise Parrish

www.ingramcontent.com/pod-product-compliance
Lightning Source LLC
Chambersburg PA
CBHW051051180526
45172CB00002B/595